Lila and Andy learn about Bridges

Revised & Updated Second Edition

Kenneth Adams

Copyright © 2025 by Kenneth Adams
All rights reserved.

No portion of this book may be reproduced in any form without written permission from the publisher or author, except as permitted by copyright law. This publication is designed to provide general information in regard to the subject matter covered. It is sold with the understanding that neither the author nor the publisher is engaged in rendering any professional services. While the publisher or author have used their best efforts in preparing this book, they make no representations or warranties with respect to the accuracy or completeness of the contents of this book and specifically disclaim any implied warranties of fitness for a particular purpose.

Book Cover by Kenneth Adams
Illustrations and Images by Kenneth Adams
Illustrations and Images created with AI Assistance
Second Edition 2025

ISBN: 978-1-998552-32-0

By overcoming our own obstacles,
we build bridges daily.

This book belongs to:

Hey there! I'm Lila, and I'm really passionate about dance and hip-hop. It's more than just a hobby for me. It's a part of who I am.

I love how I can express my feelings through movement, whether it's the sharp movements of popping, the funky grooves of locking, or going wild with freestyle. The beat of the music is like my heartbeat, pulsing through my veins and making me come alive.

I love losing myself in the rhythm and telling my story through dance.

Hi! I'm Andy. One of my many passions is cooking. I just enjoy whipping up anything from hearty Italian pastas to tasty sushi rolls. I love experimenting in the kitchen.

I'm still getting the hang of cleaning up afterwards, and I am getting better at it, but I still drive Mom mad when I sometimes leave the kitchen dirty.

My bond with my sister Lila goes beyond just being brother and sister. We're best friends who share a love for adventure. We're always challenging each other to learn more about the wonderful world around us.

Since the invention of the wheel, people have been building roads. Roads provide flat surfaces for people and vehicles to travel over land without difficulty. But what if there's a river, a valley, or even another road in the way?

Bridges were invented to solve this problem. A bridge is a structure built to cross physical barriers that would otherwise be impossible to get by. A bridge allows traffic to travel over an obstacle without blocking the path underneath.

Explore the world of bridges with Andy and me!

The type of bridge used for a specific location depends on factors such as the bridge's function, what the terrain looks like where the bridge will be constructed, how the bridge will be supported, and how much money is available to build it.

Structural engineers, like our dad, are responsible for figuring out the best type of bridge for each situation. Structural engineers design bridges to support traffic, while also making sure the bridge remains safe and sturdy for a very long time, no matter how high or how busy they are.

Here are some of the things a structural engineer thinks about when designing a bridge.

Loads: Loads are all the weight the bridge has to support without collapsing. It includes the weight of all the bridge parts, as well as the traffic passing over it.

Bridge loads are placed in different categories.

Dead loads include the weight of all the parts that make up the bridge, like the deck, beams, piers, and abutments.

Live loads are the weight of all the things that move across the bridge, all the things that come and go, like cars, trucks, and people.

Environmental loads are the forces of nature that push and pull on the bridge, like strong winds or rushing water. It also includes the weight of heavy snow and ice, and even earthquakes.

Function: This is the reason why the bridge is necessary. Will it be used for cars or for trains? Will it cross a river, a valley, or maybe even another road?

Materials: When designing a bridge, the materials you select to build the bridge with, whether concrete, steel, or wood, have to be strong enough to hold up the weight of cars and trucks and anything else that crosses the bridge. The materials should also be easy enough to acquire and move to the bridge site. You also want to select materials that will last a long time, so the bridge stays strong and safe for years to come.

Site conditions: The terrain where the bridge will be built matters when deciding what type of bridge will be best. A very deep valley will require super tall supports. A bridge over a river will require the piers to be standing in water. An engineer also has to make sure the ground is strong enough to support the bridge.

Span Length: The distance between the supports of a bridge is called the span or span length. The span is important to determine what type of bridge is most suitable. The design of bridges with longer span lengths is more complicated, while bridges with shorter spans are easier to deal with.

Bridges are built using special building blocks called <u>building materials.</u> Let's explore some of the most common ones used to create these majestic structures.

<u>Concrete</u> is a really useful material that can be used in lots of different parts of a bridge.

Concrete is made by mixing cement, sand, gravel, and water together. After mixing everything together, the concrete is poured into molds and left to dry and harden. When it's dry, concrete becomes as hard as rock and very strong!

Engineers add steel reinforcement bars to the concrete during the pouring process to make the concrete even stronger and more durable.

Concrete can be used in a couple of different ways.

<u>In situ or cast-in-place:</u> Concrete is cast, or poured, into molds at the construction site, and allowed to harden in place on the bridge. When concrete is cast in situ, it can either be mixed at the construction site or brought to the site in a concrete mixing truck.

<u>Precast:</u> Concrete is cast into molds and allowed to harden at a different location, like a factory or concrete plant. Once the concrete has sufficiently hardened, it's transported to the construction site and placed in position on the bridge.

<u>Prestressed:</u> Before the concrete is cast, strong wires or steel bars are placed in the mold. The wires are stressed by pulling the two ends of the wire apart, while the concrete is poured around it and allowed to dry and harden. The stressed wires hold the concrete together even tighter, making it stronger and able to carry more load. Prestressing can happen at the construction site, or at a factory or concrete plant.

Casting Concrete In Situ on a Bridge Deck

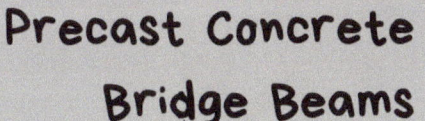

Precast Concrete Bridge Beams

Prestressed Concrete Box Beams

Steel beams form this bridge deck

A timber bridge under construction

<u>Steel</u> is another popular material used in the construction of bridges. Steel is incredibly strong and can be made into many different shapes.

This versatility allows engineers to design bridges in a variety of creative ways. Steel is also easy to work with, making the bridge construction process simpler.

<u>Timber</u> is among the oldest materials used in bridge construction. In the past, the use of wood was quite common, especially for the construction of railway bridges.

While wood is not as popular as concrete and steel nowadays, it is still widely used for the construction of shorter bridges and for bridges that are made to look nice.

People have been using <u>natural stone</u> to build bridges for thousands of years. Many of the oldest bridges in the world were originally constructed using stone.

While modern bridges are more often constructed using materials like concrete and steel, stone is still used to form bridge supports like piers and abutments for shorter bridges, bridges that don't get too much traffic, and when the bridge has to look extra pretty!

Bridges are made up of different parts that all work together to carry traffic across safely. The parts are divided into three sections: the superstructure, the substructure, and the foundation.

The <u>superstructure</u> carries the weight of the traffic that passes over the bridge. The superstructure can look different depending on the type of bridge and the materials it's made of.

The <u>substructure</u> of a bridge is the parts that support the superstructure. It transfers the loads from the superstructure down to the bridge foundation.

The <u>foundation</u> is the part that is underground. It supports the bridge by spreading the bridge and traffic loads evenly over the supporting soil, preventing the bridge from sinking into the ground.

The Superstructure

The superstructure consists of the following main elements:

<u>Pylons and Towers:</u> These are the tall vertical structures built along the length of the bridge. They extend above the bridge deck and support the cables from which the deck is suspended. Pylons are commonly associated with cable-stayed bridges and tend to be more slender, while towers are associated with suspension bridges and may appear more bulky. Both transfer the weight of the deck through the cables down to the foundation, and are typically made of steel or concrete.

<u>Bridge Deck:</u> The deck is the flat surface at the top of the bridge. It carries the roadway that traffic, like vehicles and pedestrians, can use to travel on.

<u>Girders:</u> These are horizontal elements that support the deck. Girders are a type of rigid beam that can carry large loads. They are usually located just below the deck and are made of steel or concrete.

<u>Trusses:</u> Similar to girders, trusses are horizontal elements that support the deck. Trusses consist of a framework of elements, connected together to form a sturdy, stable structure. Trusses are commonly fabricated using structural steel sections.

Bridge Towers

Section through a bridge deck

A steel plate girder

Steel Trusses

The Superstructure

<u>Cables:</u> The large cables that support the weight of the bridge deck on suspension and cable-stayed bridges are made by tightly binding together high-strength steel wires. The size of the cable is determined by the loads it needs to support.

<u>Bearings:</u> When traffic travels over a bridge deck, it causes tiny movements in the deck, while the supports remain still. Bridge bearings are placed between the bridge deck and the bridge supports to allow the deck to move without damaging the supports.

<u>Expansion Joints:</u> Bridges are exposed to the elements, and expand and contract as the ambient temperature changes. Expansion joints are gaps in the bridge deck that allow the deck to change in size during expansion or contraction, without causing damage to the deck or the supports.

<u>Drainage:</u> Pooling water can lead to damage to structural elements on a bridge by causing corrosion or deterioration of the deck. All bridges include systems that drain water off the bridge to prevent damage and improve road safety.

The Substructure

The substructure consists of the following main elements:

<u>Piers:</u> These are the vertical support structures that are located along the length of the bridge. They are often constructed in the water or in the middle of a long span. Piers typically sit below the bridge deck, and can be made of concrete, steel, or natural stone.

<u>Abutments:</u> These are the bridge support structures at each end of the bridge, where the bridge meets the land. They consist of walls that transfer the weight of the bridge to the ground, and are typically made of concrete or natural stone.

The Foundation

<u>Foundations:</u> At the bottom of each bridge support structure is an underground structure called a foundation. Foundations are designed to spread the weight of the bridge over a large area of ground or rock. Foundations are most often made from concrete, but can also be made from steel or wood.

Bridge Piers

A Bridge Abutment

A Pier Foundation being Constructed in Water

Bridges come in many different types, and sometimes engineers combine different types to make really unique bridges. Engineers are always dreaming up new, innovative, and better bridge designs, too! Let's check out the most popular types used today.

Ready to see some awesome bridges? Let's go!

Arch Bridge

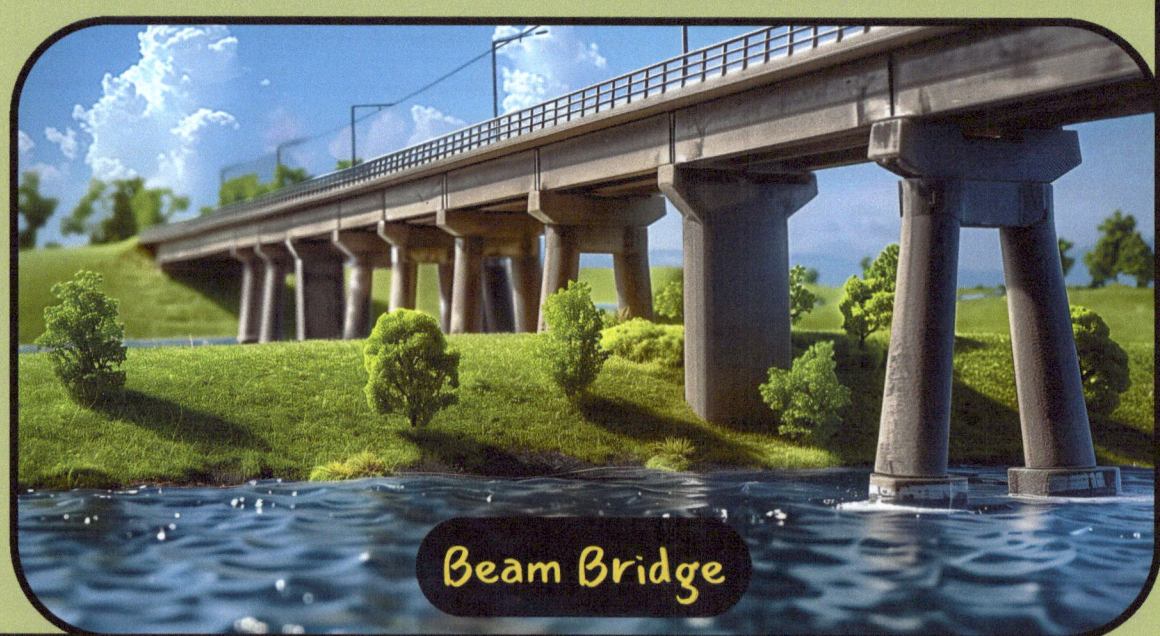
Beam Bridge

Arch Bridges

An arch is a curved structure supported on both ends.

An arch bridge uses the strength of the curved shape to hold up the bridge deck, while the weight of the bridge and the traffic that passes over it are pushed down to the ground through the abutments at both ends of the arch.

Beam Bridges

Beam bridges are the simplest form of bridge. A beam is a long, slender, horizontal structural element that stretches across an opening, while being supported at each end, carrying loads in a direction perpendicular to its length.

Beam bridges are relatively cheap to construct and are most often used for bridges with shorter spans.

A cantilever bridge under construction

Cantilever Bridges

Cantilever bridges have long arms called cantilevers that extend outward from a single support point, like a pier. Cantilevers only need support on one end, while the other end is left with no support.

To construct a cantilever bridge, two cantilevers are constructed, one from each side of the river or valley. The cantilevers meet in the middle to create the main part of the bridge.

On smaller pedestrian bridges, simple beams are used for the cantilevers. On larger bridges that carry vehicle traffic, the cantilevers can be made from trusses built from structural steel, or from steel or prestressed concrete box girders.

The cantilevers work together to support the weight of the bridge deck and any traffic passing over it. The load is transferred through the cantilevers to the supporting piers or abutments, from where it passes to the ground through the foundation.

Steel Girder Bridge

A concrete box girder fabricated on site

Girder Bridges

This type of bridge is supported by large, rigid beams known as girders. Girders are fabricated to be very strong, and girder bridges are relatively simple to construct.

Concrete girders can be made from cast-in-place, precast, or prestressed concrete.

Rolled steel girders are made from a single piece of steel, usually in the shape of an "I", while plate girders are made by welding together multiple steel plates into very strong sections.

Box Girder Bridges

A box girder bridge, or box section bridge, is a type of bridge in which the main beams are made of girders in the shape of a hollow box.

Box girders are commonly made from prestressed concrete, structural steel, or a combination of steel and reinforced concrete. The cross-section of the box is typically rectangular or trapezoidal.

Suspension Bridges

The word "suspend" means to hang something from somewhere. On suspension bridges, the bridge deck is hung off vertical suspender or hanger cables, which are supported by two larger cables.

The larger cables are suspended between tall towers and are anchored at each end of the bridge. The weight of the bridge and the traffic passing over it is carried over to the towers through the cables.

Suspension bridges can span very long distances, and are often used for crossings over large bodies of water.

Cable-stayed Bridges

On cable-stayed bridges, the bridge deck is supported by cables that are attached directly to the pylons of the bridge.

Unlike suspension bridges with their hanging cables, cable-stayed bridges have cables that go straight from the bridge deck to the tall supports.

On cable-stayed bridges, the weight of the bridge and the traffic passing over it is carried to the pylons through the cables.

Cable-stayed bridges are less expensive to build than suspension bridges, and are ideal for spans shorter than suspension bridges.

Tied-arch Bridges

Similar to an arch bridge, a tied-arch bridge uses the strength of a curved shape, an arch, to hold up the weight of the road and the traffic passing over it. However, instead of the loads being pushed down to the ground through the abutments, the ends of the arch are tied together by a chord.

This chord, or tie, may be the bridge deck itself, or it could be a separate, independent tie-rod. The 'tie' helps the bridge stay strong and keeps the ends of the curve from spreading apart.

Picture a bow and arrow, where the ends of the curved bow are tied together by the bow string. When you try to flatten the curved bow, the bow string will go into tension and will try to prevent the ends of the bow from moving away from each other.

Trestle Bridge

Truss Bridge

Trestle Bridges

Trestle bridges are built with a series of short spans supported by frames that are placed close to each other. A trestle bridge looks like a super-long table with lots of legs.

Trestle bridges made of timber were often used for railways crossing valleys or gorges, but they can also be constructed using steel or sometimes concrete.

Truss Bridges

On this type of bridge, the superstructure carrying the loads is formed using trusses.

A truss is a framework of connected structural elements working together to distribute the weight of the bridge and the traffic evenly to the supports.

Trusses are strong and can be made in a variety of different forms to span longer distances than beam bridges.

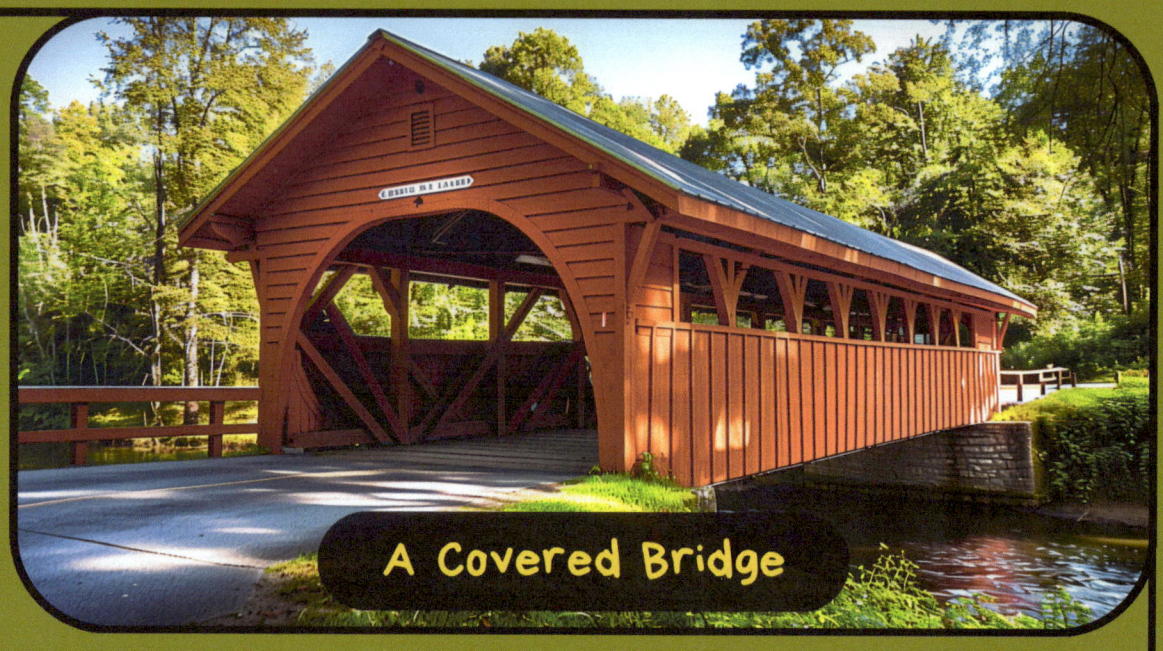

A Covered Bridge

A Stressed Ribbon Bridge

Covered Bridges

Most covered bridges are timber bridges that have a roof and walls over the roadway. The bridges are covered to protect the wood from deterioration because of exposure to the elements.

Covered bridges aren't built much anymore, and the older ones that still exist are mostly seen as historic landmarks.

Stressed Ribbon Bridges

Stressed ribbon bridges function similarly to simple suspension bridges, but instead of the superstructure hanging off the suspension cables, the cables are built into the bridge deck.

The cables are stressed by pulling the ends of the cables apart, "pulling" the concrete deck tight together. This makes the deck stiffer, making it stronger and able to carry more loads.

Stressed ribbon bridges are typically made from concrete, reinforced by steel tensioning cables, and are often used for footbridges in parks because they look nice.

A Drawbridge

A Pontoon Bridge being moved into place

Movable Bridges

Movable bridges are bridges that can be raised or lowered to allow for the passage of tall ships or other vessels.

There are many different types of movable bridges. The superstructure can be made to swing upwards, like a drawbridge, or the entire span can lift vertically.

Another example of a moving bridge is a swing bridge, where the deck is made to rotate around a vertical axis.

Pontoon Bridges

Pontoon bridges are bridges that are supported by a series of specialized floating platforms, or pontoons. They are also called floating bridges.

Pontoon bridges are easy to build and can be moved around, so technically, they can also be considered a movable bridge. They are not very strong and cannot span long distances.

They are often used by the military during wartime, and they're also super helpful when there's a flood and we need a quick bridge.

A Roman Aqueduct

A Viaduct runs through a valley

Aqueduct

This is a special kind of bridge that carries water instead of cars or trains! The ancient Romans built many aqueducts to bring water to their cities.

Today, we still use them to move water across valleys or rivers, and larger aqueducts are navigable by boats.

Viaducts

A viaduct is a long bridge that carries a road or railway across a very wide valley. It consists of many spans and piers. Think of it as a bridge that looks like it has lots of legs to stand on.

Viaducts can differ greatly in design and materials, incorporating features such as arches, trusses, or beams, based on the engineering needs and desired aesthetics.

Wow! We learned so much about bridges today! We learned what a bridge is, we learned about the different types of bridges, and even what they are made of.

Who knew there were so many kinds of bridges? They're also not just for cars and people. Some bridges carry trains, and aqueducts even carry water!

Next time you see a bridge on your way to school, try to impress your friends by naming its type. You're a bridge expert now!

Bridge Careers

If you care about connecting our communities safely while respecting the environment, then careers dedicated to bridge engineering and construction might be perfect for you! There are many exciting jobs for people who want to help create the structures that span rivers, valleys, and obstacles to connect our neighborhoods, schools, and businesses. Here are examples of careers that work together to build every bridge we need while protecting our natural landscapes and waterways for future generations.

Engineering Planning & Design:

- Structural Engineer - Designs the bridge framework and calculates how much weight it can safely carry. They determine which materials to use and how to design the bridge to ensure it is strong enough.

- Civil Engineer - Plans the overall bridge project, including where it should go and how it connects to roads.

- Geotechnical Engineer - Studies the soil and rock where the bridge will be built to make sure the ground is strong enough to support the bridge foundations.

- Transportation Engineer - Plans how traffic will flow on and around the bridge, and designs the road connections on both sides.

- Architect - Focuses on making the bridge visually appealing while working with engineers to ensure it remains functional and safe.

- <u>Hydrologist</u> - Studies water flow, flooding patterns, and how the bridge might affect rivers or streams underneath.

- <u>Environmental Engineer</u> - Ensures that bridge construction and design won't harm plants, animals, or the surrounding environment.

- <u>Surveyor</u> - Uses special tools to measure the land precisely and create detailed maps showing where the bridge will be built.

Construction:

- <u>Construction Contractor/General Contractor</u> - The company or person hired to build the bridge. They coordinate all the different workers and subcontractors needed to complete the project.

- <u>Construction Manager</u> - Oversees the entire bridge-building process, making sure work is done safely, on time, and correctly.

- <u>Project Manager</u> - Manages the schedule, budget, and coordinates all the different workers and materials needed to build the bridge.

- <u>Heavy Equipment Operator</u> - Operates big machines like bulldozers, excavators, and other equipment used in construction.

- <u>Crane Operator</u> - Controls the large cranes that lift and place heavy bridge parts like steel beams and concrete sections.

- <u>Concrete Worker</u> - Mixes, pours, and shapes concrete for bridge foundations, decks, and other concrete parts.

- <u>Steel Worker/Iron Worker</u> - Assembles and installs the steel beams, girders, and other metal parts that form the bridge structure.

Maintenance and Operations:

- <u>Bridge Inspector</u> - Regularly checks bridges for cracks, rust, or other problems to make sure they stay safe for everyone to use.

- <u>Maintenance Engineer</u> - Plans what repairs or maintenance work needs to be done and figures out the best way to do it.

- <u>Bridge Maintenance Worker</u> - Does the actual repair and maintenance work, like painting, fixing cracks, and replacing damaged and old parts.

Bridges Glossary

A <u>glossary</u> is like a mini-dictionary of terms with definitions.
Here's a glossary of terms associated with <u>Bridges</u>.

<u>Abutment</u> - The support structure at each end of a bridge where it meets the land.

<u>Aqueduct</u> - A special type of bridge designed to carry water instead of vehicles or people.

<u>Arch</u> - A curved structure that supports weight by pushing forces down to its ends.

<u>Arch Bridge</u> - A bridge that uses curved arches to support the deck and transfer weight to the ground.

<u>Beam</u> - A long, horizontal structural piece that spans across an opening and carries loads.

<u>Beam Bridge</u> - The simplest type of bridge, made of beams supported at each end.

<u>Bearings</u> - Special connections between the bridge deck and supports that allow small movements.

<u>Box Girder</u> - A type of beam shaped like a hollow box, which makes it very strong.

<u>Bridge Deck</u> - The flat surface on top of a bridge where traffic travels.

<u>Cable</u> - Strong steel wires bundled together to support suspension and cable-stayed bridges.

<u>Cable-Stayed Bridge</u> - A bridge where the deck is supported by cables attached directly to tall towers.

<u>Cantilever</u> - A beam or structure supported at only one end, with the other end free.

<u>Cantilever Bridge</u> - A bridge built using two cantilevers that extend toward each other from opposite sides.

<u>Cast in Place</u> - Concrete that is poured and allowed to harden at the construction site.

Concrete - A building material made from cement, sand, gravel, and water that hardens like rock.

Covered Bridge - A bridge with a roof and walls, usually made of wood, to protect it from weather.

Dead Load - The weight of the bridge itself, including all its permanent parts.

Drainage - Systems that move water off the bridge to prevent damage and improve safety.

Environmental Load - Forces from nature that act on bridges, like wind, earthquakes, or snow.

Expansion Joint - Gaps in the bridge deck that allow it to expand and contract with temperature changes.

Foundation - The underground part of bridge supports that spreads the bridge's weight over the ground.

Girder - A large, strong beam used to support the bridge deck.

Girder Bridge - A bridge supported by large, rigid beams called girders.

In Situ - Another term for "cast in place" concrete work.

Live Load - The weight of moving things on the bridge, like cars, trucks, and people.

Load - Any weight or force that the bridge must support.

Movable Bridge - A bridge that can be raised, lowered, or moved to allow ships to pass.

Pier - A vertical support structure built along the length of a bridge, often in water.

Pontoon Bridge - A floating bridge supported by special platforms called pontoons.

Precast - Concrete parts made at a factory and then transported to the bridge site.

Prestressed - Concrete that is made extra strong by stretching steel wires or cables inside it.

Pylon - A tall, slender tower that supports the cables on a cable-stayed bridge.

Reinforcement - Steel bars added to concrete to make it stronger.

Span - The distance between two bridge supports; also refers to the section of bridge between supports.

Steel - A very strong metal material used in bridge construction.

Stressed Ribbon Bridge - A bridge where cables are built into the concrete deck to make it stronger.

Substructure - The parts of a bridge below the deck that support it, including piers and abutments.

Superstructure - The parts of a bridge above the supports, including the deck and beams.

Suspension Bridge - A bridge where the deck hangs from cables supported by tall towers.

Suspender Cable - The vertical cables that hang the deck from the main cables on suspension bridges.

Tied-Arch Bridge - An arch bridge where the ends of the arch are connected by a tie to prevent spreading.

Timber - Wood used as a building material for bridges.

Tower - A tall, sturdy structure that supports the main cables on a suspension bridge.

Trestle Bridge - A bridge built with many short spans supported by closely-spaced frames.

Truss - A framework of connected pieces that work together to support loads.

Truss Bridge - A bridge where the main support structure is made of connected framework pieces.

Viaduct - A long bridge with many spans that carries roads or railways across wide valleys.

Bridges Quiz

Multiple Choice (Choose the best answer)

1. What is a bridge?
   a) A road that goes underground
   b) A structure built to cross physical barriers
   c) A type of building material
   d) A tool used by engineers

2. Which type of load includes the weight of cars and trucks on a bridge?
   a) Dead load
   b) Live load
   c) Environmental load
   d) Static load

3. What material is made by mixing cement, sand, gravel, and water?
   a) Steel
   b) Timber
   c) Concrete
   d) Stone

4. Which bridge type uses curved shapes to transfer weight to the ground?
   a) Suspension bridge
   b) Arch bridge
   c) Beam bridge
   d) Cable-stayed bridge

5. What is the flat surface on top of a bridge called?
   a) Superstructure
   b) Foundation
   c) Bridge deck
   d) Substructure

6. Which professional studies soil and rock conditions for bridge construction?
   a) Civil engineer
   b) Structural engineer
   c) Geotechnical engineer
   d) Environmental engineer

7. What type of bridge hangs its deck from cables supported by tall towers?
   a) Arch bridge
   b) Beam bridge
   c) Suspension bridge
   d) Truss bridge

8. Which bridge part is underground and spreads the bridge's weight?
   a) Pier
   b) Abutment
   c) Deck
   d) Foundation

9. What are the vertical support structures along a bridge's length called?
   a) Abutments
   b) Piers
   c) Foundations
   d) Girders

10. Which type of concrete is poured and hardened at the construction site?
    a) Precast
    b) Prestressed
    c) Cast in place
    d) Reinforced

11. What do bridge inspectors look for during their examinations?
    a) Traffic patterns
    b) Cracks, rust, and other problems
    c) New construction materials
    d) Weather conditions

12. Which bridge type looks like a table with many legs?
    a) Suspension bridge
    b) Arch bridge
    c) Trestle bridge
    d) Cable-stayed bridge

13. What is the distance between bridge supports called?
    a) Length
    b) Width
    c) Height
    d) Span

14. Which material was commonly used for railway bridges in the past?
    a) Concrete
    b) Steel
    c) Timber
    d) Stone

15. What type of bridge carries water instead of vehicles?
    a) Viaduct
    b) Pontoon bridge
    c) Aqueduct
    d) Covered bridge

16. Which forces are considered environmental loads?
    a) Car weight
    b) Bridge material weight
    c) Wind and earthquakes
    d) Pedestrian weight

17. What connects the bridge deck to the supports and allows small movements?
    a) Expansion joints
    b) Bearings
    c) Cables
    d) Drainage systems

18. Which bridge type has cables attached directly to tall towers?
    a) Suspension bridge
    b) Cable-stayed bridge
    c) Arch bridge
    d) Beam bridge

19. What are the support structures at each end of a bridge called?
    a) Piers
    b) Foundations
    c) Abutments
    d) Towers

20. Which professional operates large cranes during construction?
    a) Steel worker
    b) Concrete worker
    c) Crane operator
    d) Heavy equipment operator

21. What type of bridge can be raised or lowered for ships?
    a) Fixed bridge
    b) Movable bridge
    c) Permanent bridge
    d) Solid bridge

22. Which bridge component prevents water damage and improves safety?
    a) Expansion joints
    b) Bearings
    c) Drainage systems
    d) Cables

23. What makes prestressed concrete stronger than regular concrete?
    a) More cement
    b) Stretched steel wires inside
    c) Thicker sections
    d) Better mixing

24. Which bridge type uses a framework of connected structural elements?
    a) Beam bridge
    b) Arch bridge
    c) Truss bridge
    d) Girder bridge

25. What do environmental engineers ensure during bridge projects?
    a) Traffic flows smoothly
    b) Materials are strong enough
    c) The environment isn't harmed
    d) Construction stays on schedule

Fill-in-the-Blank

26. The three main sections of a bridge are the superstructure, substructure, and _____.

27. _____ bridges are supported by special floating platforms.

28. The _____ carries the roadway that traffic uses to travel on.

29. A _____ is a beam or structure supported at only one end.

30. _____ concrete is cast into molds at a factory before being transported to the site.

31. The _____ of a bridge includes piers and abutments.

32. _____ loads include the weight of heavy snow, ice, and wind.

33. A _____ engineer plans how traffic will flow on and around the bridge.

34. _____ bridges have a roof and walls to protect the wood from weather.

35. The ancient _____ built many aqueducts to bring water to their cities.

36. A _____ is a long bridge with many spans that crosses wide valleys.

37. _____ are gaps in the bridge deck that allow it to expand and contract.

38. Steel _____ bars are added to concrete to make it stronger.

39. A _____ bridge uses two cantilevers that extend toward each other from opposite sides.

40. The _____ is responsible for figuring out the best type of bridge for each situation.

41. _____ bridges are the simplest form of bridge design.

42. A box _____ is shaped like a hollow box and is very strong.

43. _____ cables hang the deck from the main cables on suspension bridges.

44. The terrain where a bridge will be built affects the _____ conditions.

45. _____ are used to measure land precisely and create detailed construction maps.

46. A tied-arch bridge has its arch ends connected by a _____.

47. _____ workers mix, pour, and shape concrete for bridge construction.

48. The _____ manages the schedule and budget for bridge projects.

49. Bridge _____ regularly check bridges for safety problems.

50. _____ is among the oldest materials used in bridge construction.

True/False (Write T for True or F for False)

51. Dead loads include the weight of cars and trucks crossing the bridge. _____

52. Suspension bridges can span very long distances. _____

53. All bridges must have piers in the middle of their spans. _____

54. Steel is easy to work with during bridge construction. _____

55. Covered bridges are built frequently in modern times. _____

56. Environmental loads include the effects of earthquakes. _____

57. Beam bridges are the most complex type of bridge to build. _____

58. Abutments are located at each end of a bridge. _____

59. Pontoon bridges are very strong and can span long distances. _____

60. Prestressing makes concrete weaker than regular concrete. _____

61. Viaducts consist of many spans and piers. _____

62. Bridge bearings prevent the deck from moving. _____

63. Cast-in-place concrete is mixed and poured at the construction site. _____

64. Cable-stayed bridges cost more to build than suspension bridges. _____

65. Trestle bridges look like tables with many legs. _____

66. Stone is still used for some modern bridge construction. _____

67. Expansion joints allow bridges to change size with temperature. _____

68. Hydrologists study traffic patterns for bridge planning. _____

69. Box girders can be made from both steel and concrete. _____

70. Stressed ribbon bridges are commonly used for footbridges in parks. _____

Quiz Answer Key

Multiple Choice	Fill-in-the-Blank	True/False
1. b	26. foundation	51. False
2. b	27. Pontoon	52. True
3. c	28. bridge deck	53. False
4. b	29. cantilever	54. True
5. c	30. Precast	55. False
6. c	31. substructure	56. True
7. c	32. Environmental	57. False
8. d	33. Transportation	58. True
9. b	34. Covered	59. False
10. c	35. Romans	60. False
11. b	36. viaduct	61. True
12. c	37. Expansion joints	62. False
13. d	38. reinforcement	63. True
14. c	39. cantilever	64. False
15. c	40. structural engineer	65. True
16. c	41. Beam	66. True
17. b	42. girder	67. True
18. b	43. Suspender	68. False
19. c	44. site	69. True
20. c	45. Surveyors	70. True
21. b	46. tie	
22. c	47. Concrete	
23. b	48. project manager	
24. c	49. inspectors	
25. c	50. Timber	

Take a look at other subjects Lila and Andy are learning about...

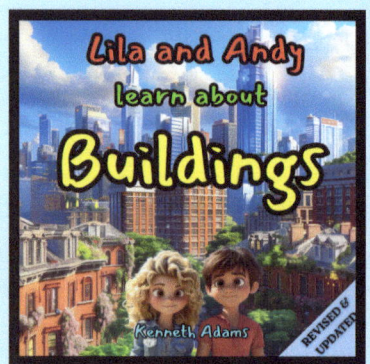
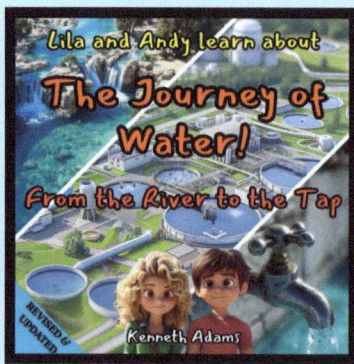
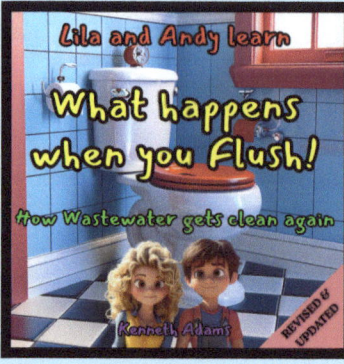
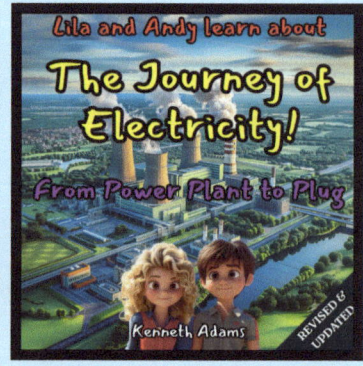

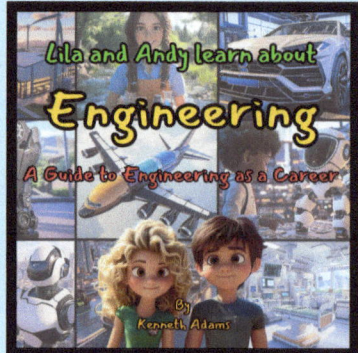
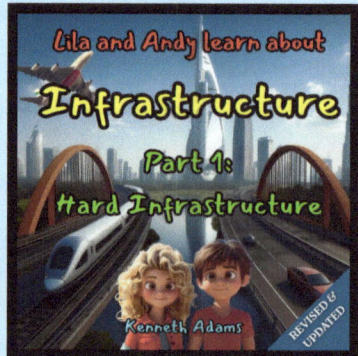
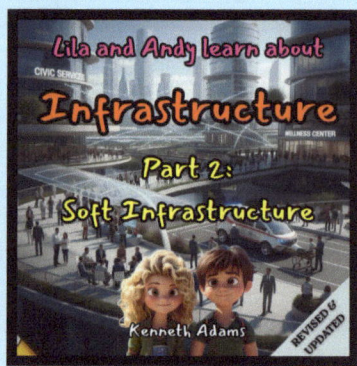
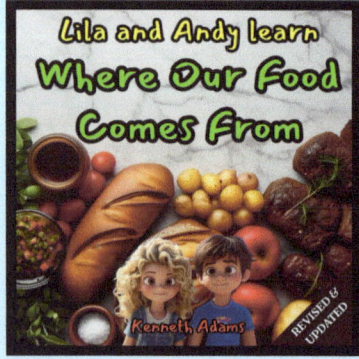
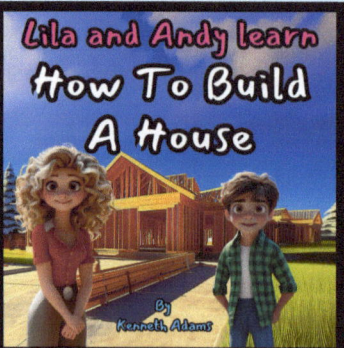
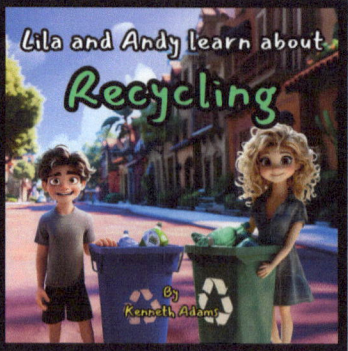

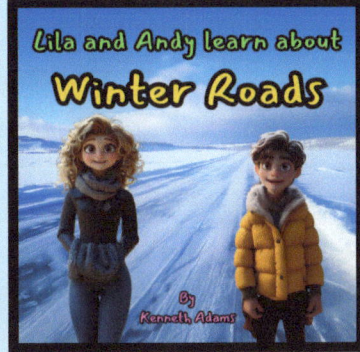

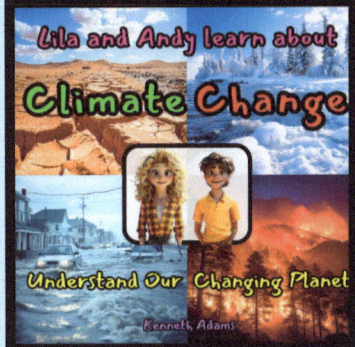

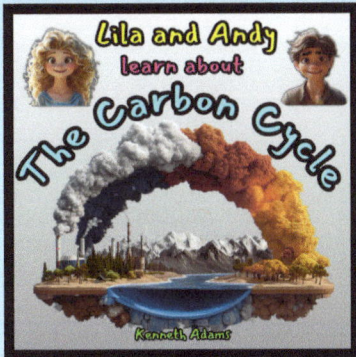

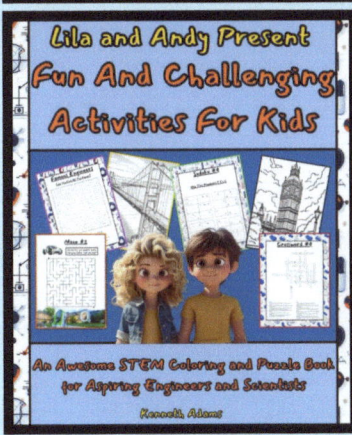
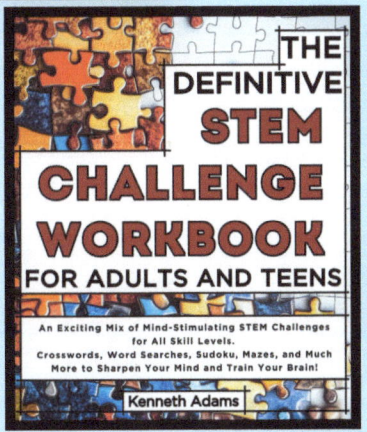
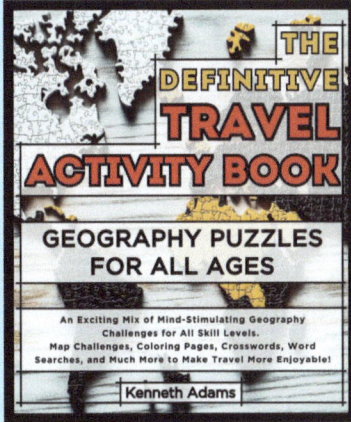

www.ingramcontent.com/pod-product-compliance
Lightning Source LLC
Chambersburg PA
CBHW042022080426
42735CB00003B/132